DESERT RAIN

A Wild Horizons™ Postcard Book

Photography by Thomas A. Wiewandt
Introduction by John Alcock

WILD HORIZONS PUBLISHING, INC.
TUCSON, ARIZONA

Series Editor: Thomas Wiewandt
Design: Paul Mirocha
Production: Ejyo Katagiri
Copy Editing: Sally Antrobus-Wilkinson,
 Jeffrey H. Lockridge
Author's Bio: Deborah Mitchell
Scientific Consultant:
 Dr. Mark Dimmitt,
 Arizona-Sonora Desert Museum

Publisher's Cataloging-in-Publication Data:

Wiewandt, Thomas A.
DESERT RAIN/DESERT BLOOM:
 A Wild Horizons Postcard Book

ISBN 1-879728-00-1

1. Desert ecology, Southwest, New—pictorial works.
2. Desert plants, Southwest, New—pictorial works.
3. Weather, arid lands—pictorial works.
4. Wildflowers, desert—pictorial works. I. Title
 QH or TR

First Edition, 1992, Printed in Singapore 7 6 5 4 3 2 1

Wild Horizons Publishing
Post Office Box 5118-00
Tucson, Arizona 85703-0118
U.S.A.

For more Wild Horizons™ books, try your local bookstores, use the order card in the rear of this book, call toll free: 1-800-969-9558, or send a FAX: 602-624-5888.

RHYTHMS IN AN ARID LAND

A TOWERING WALL OF of dust spreads across the desert, swallowing up the giant cacti and the scruffy desert trees. Gritty winds swirl wildly among the plants. It has been months since the last rain. The punishing heat of summer has held complete dominance for so long that the memory of rainfall seems illusory. And now the dust storm sweeps in to draw the last moisture from the stoic plants. It blows a handful of dry, gray leaflets from a hollow beneath the ironwood where they fell long ago. They skitter across an empty streamed that flows with sand, not water.

But in the distance comes a rumble of thunder and then another, a slashing rip of lightning, the first plump drops of rain. At first isolated and filled with dust, the drops now descend in droves, washing the air clean, thumping into the sand of the dry wash, streaking and then cleansing the immense saguaro cacti and the little twisted bursage shrubs alike. The summer rains have arrived at last; hidden in the final dust storm of the season, the wonderful downpour brings with it the distillation of relief.

In the desert Southwest of the United States, rains come sparingly during a summer monsoon season that may begin as early as June or as late as August before ending in September. The monsoon rainstorms roar into the desert from the south, accompanied by swollen thunderheads, riotous winds, lightning, and dust. The storms dispense their moisture capriciously, bestowing a deluge on one patch of desert and only a sprinkle on another close by.

Within the deluge, water spills down so quickly that the soil cannot accommodate it all. The excess water slips down hillsides and slides off rock walls, forming rivulets that coalesce and gather strength before they enter the main drainages, most of which were bone-dry before the storm. Water and soil mingle together and surge downward and across the desert flats, at first rambunctiously, then more tamely, until at last the water sinks beneath the sand.

A second rainy season occurs during the winter, when rainfall arrives with a serenity that is the exact opposite of the uncontrolled exuberance of a monsoon storm. Thick, somber clouds slowly fill the sky from horizon to horizon. They parcel out their moisture in drizzles, mists, fogs, and sometimes snow, over hours or days rather than minutes. The land absorbs the winter rain by degrees, savoring each droplet.

The combined rainfall from both wild monsoon and sedate winter storms does not exceed 10 inches (25 centimeters) per year over much of the western United States. Even so, a great diversity of plants has succeeded in colonizing these deserts: the Sonoran, the Chihuahuan, the Great Basin, and the Mojave. Desert plants succeed because they have invented a variety of tactics to adapt to the formidable aridity of the landscape.

Some, like the sheltering honey mesquite, grow by washes where the water table is closest to the surface, although still far below ground. The mesquite trees send down long taproots many meters deep into the soil in search of reliable water, which sustains their predictable annual cycle of leaf production and flowering, followed by near dormancy during the hottest part of the year.

Others, like the huge saguaro, grow on desert flats and rocky hillsides, where they spread out a fine net of shallow roots to intercept any moisture that reaches them just after rainfall. The saguaro and other cacti store the water they glean from the soil within their fleshy bodies for later use. In so doing, these succulent plants of the desert achieve a certain independence from the annual fluctuations in rainfall. They usually manage to flower each year and some, like the saguaro, even thumb their noses at the brutal heat of summer by flowering at the height of the drought in May and June.

Still others, especially the ephemeral annuals, depend utterly on end-of-the-year precipitation. In the Mojave Desert, unusually good rains must fall after the dog days of summer but before the winter freezes if a banner-year bloom of annuals is to occur. But when they do (perhaps one year in ten), desert poppies, lupines, and owl-clovers germinate in great density and grow shoulder to shoulder in places. When spring comes, the little annuals open their flowers by the thousands, combining to create enchanted mosaics of color on the desert floor as they race to reproduce before the drought of late spring kills them. Those that succeed leave a legacy of seeds to wait, often for years, for the next perfectly timed combination of autumn storms to trigger a new cycle of growth, flowering, seed production, and death.

Thus, despite the inhospitable climate of the deserts in the American West, we can celebrate the diversity of life found there as well as the drama of the seasons, the hope produced by rain in places that really appreciate it, and the vitality of desert plants that do more than just survive under the handicaps they confront each day.

— JOHN ALCOCK

. . . .
John Alcock is a professor of zoology at Arizona State University in Tempe, Arizona. Among his recent books are *Sonoran Desert Spring* (1985), *The Kookaburras' Song: Exploring Animal Behavior in Australia* (1988), and *Sonoran Desert Summer* (1990).

SUNLIGHT OFTEN MEETS rain in deserts of the American Southwest, creating kaleidoscopic moments of unsurpassed beauty. This rainbow graces a saguaro-studded landscape in the Tucson Mountains of the Sonoran Desert, southern Arizona. (100)

From *DESERT RAIN/DESERT BLOOM*, a Wild Horizons Postcard Book, P.O. Box 5118–00, Tucson, Arizona 85703–0118 USA
Photo © 1991 by Thomas Wiewandt.

*I*N EARLY SPRING, poppies (*Eschscholtzia californica* — California's state flower) and goldfields (*Lasthenia chrysotoma*) paint the Mojave desert in brilliant orange and yellow. Brief but spectacular shows of this intensity occur in Antelope Valley once every several years, seen here amongst sagebrush and Joshua trees (*Yucca brevifolia*). (200)

From *DESERT RAIN/DESERT BLOOM*, a Wild Horizons Postcard Book, P.O. Box 5118–00, Tucson, Arizona 85703–0118 USA
Photo © 1991 by Thomas Wiewandt.

S CORPIONWEED BLOSSOMS (*Phacelia* sp.) poke through a white bursage (*Franseria dumosa*) in the Mojave Desert of Joshua Tree National Monument, California. (300)

From *DESERT RAIN*/*DESERT BLOOM*, a Wild Horizons Postcard Book, P.O. Box 5118–00, Tucson, Arizona 85703–0118 USA
Photo © 1991 by Thomas Wiewandt.

*F*OLLOWING AN EXCEPTIONALLY moist and mild winter, fragrant evening primroses (*Oenothera deltoides*) and purple sand verbenas (*Abronia villosa*) embellish dunes that flank Joshua Tree National Monument, California. In the background, a desert lily (*Hesperocallis undulata*) sends up its flowering stalk. (400)

From *DESERT RAIN/DESERT BLOOM*, a Wild Horizons Postcard Book, P.O. Box 5118–00, Tucson, Arizona 85703–0118 USA
Photo © 1991 by Thomas Wiewandt.

I N SPRING, LUPINES (*Lupinus sparsiflorus*) and hedgehog cacti (*Echinocereus fasciculatus*) bloom side by side on the Tohono O'odham reservation in southern Arizona. While desert lupines make only a fleeting appearance at best, cacti store enough water and food to flower nearly every year. (500)

From *DESERT RAIN/DESERT BLOOM*, a Wild Horizons Postcard Book, P.O. Box 5118–00, Tucson, Arizona 85703–0118 USA
Photo © 1991 by Thomas Wiewandt.

*D*ESERT TRUMPET FLOWERS (*Eriogonum inflatum*) are so tiny they rarely attract attention; but the plant's striking, curvaceous stems are of both aesthetic and scientific interest. In the southern reaches of the Great Basin Desert, these plants have swollen stems, apparently caused by the feeding activities and secretions of moth larvae within. (600)

From *DESERT RAIN/DESERT BLOOM*, a Wild Horizons Postcard Book, P.O. Box 5118–00, Tucson, Arizona 85703–0118 USA
Photo © 1991 by Thomas Wiewandt.

A SEEMINGLY ENDLESS field of poppies (*Eschscholtzia californica*) and goldenbush (*Haplopappus* sp.) transforms California's Antelope Valley into a fantasyland. In early spring, these poppies rush to bloom and set seed in two or three weeks, before the hot, dry weather begins. (700)

From *DESERT RAIN/DESERT BLOOM*, a Wild Horizons Postcard Book, P.O. Box 5118–00, Tucson, Arizona 85703–0118 USA
Photo © 1991 by Thomas Wiewandt.

A SPRINGTIME TAPESTRY of owl-clover (*Orthocarpus purpurascens*) and lupine (*Lupinus sparsiflorus*) enlivens a patch of Sonoran Desert on the Tohono O'odham reservation of southern Arizona. (800)

From *DESERT RAIN/DESERT BLOOM*, a Wild Horizons Postcard Book, P.O. Box 5118–00, Tucson, Arizona 85703–0118 USA
Photo © 1991 by Thomas Wiewandt.

A GRAVELLY SLOPE IN Death Valley National Monument bristles with desert dandelions (*Malacothrix californica*). Closely related to the common dandelion and chicory, this is one of the most common spring wildflowers in arid lands of the American Southwest. (900)

From *DESERT RAIN/DESERT BLOOM*, a Wild Horizons Postcard Book, P.O. Box 5118–00, Tucson, Arizona 85703–0118 USA
Photo © 1991 by Thomas Wiewandt.

SUMMER MOISTURE often makes its first appearance in the American Southwest as *virga*, a phantom rain that trails from clouds but evaporates before it reaches the ground. (1000)

From *DESERT RAIN/DESERT BLOOM*, a Wild Horizons Postcard Book, P.O. Box 5118–00, Tucson, Arizona 85703–0118 USA
Photo © 1991 by Thomas Wiewandt.

A MULTIPLE STRIKE of cloud-to-ground lightning illuminates the Tucson Mountain skyline near Gates Pass. Lightning expends much energy in an incredibly brief period of time, spanning only millionths to thousandths of a second. The current is so concentrated— in a path only a few inches wide— that the air within reaches temperatures several times hotter than the surface of the sun. (1300)

From *DESERT RAIN/DESERT BLOOM*, a Wild Horizons Postcard Book, P.O. Box 5118–00, Tucson, Arizona 85703–0118 USA
Photo © 1991 by Thomas Wiewandt.

As a nighttime rainstorm sweeps through Saguaro National Monument, the sky flickers with lightning, much of which stays airborne. Thunder results from the explosive heating of air along the length of a lightning flash. How loud it is depends upon the intensity of the flash, distance, and atmospheric conditions. (1200)

From *Desert Rain/Desert Bloom*, a Wild Horizons Postcard Book, P.O. Box 5118–00, Tucson, Arizona 85703–0118 USA
Photo © 1991 by Thomas Wiewandt.

S HORTLY AFTER SUNSET, alpenglow and lightning illuminate an enormous thunderhead, prelude to a summer monsoon rainstorm in southern Arizona. One flash strikes the ground, while another discharges across the cloud's crown. (1100)

From *DESERT RAIN/DESERT BLOOM*, a Wild Horizons Postcard Book, P.O. Box 5118–00, Tucson, Arizona 85703–0118 USA
Photo © 1991 by Thomas Wiewandt.

Called "WALKING RAIN" by Native Americans, a small, fast-moving rainstorm has formed over the Roskruge Mountains of southern Arizona. This astonishing sunset with a lightning strike and clouds in motion was photographed using an eight-second exposure. (1400)

From *DESERT RAIN/DESERT BLOOM*, a Wild Horizons Postcard Book, P.O. Box 5118–00, Tucson, Arizona 85703–0118 USA
Photo © 1991 by Thomas Wiewandt.

A RAINDROP CLINGS to a spine of the fishhook barrel cactus (*Ferocactus wislizenii*), a native of the Chihuahuan and Sonoran Deserts, ranging from Mexico and southern Texas west into Arizona. (1600)

From *DESERT RAIN/DESERT BLOOM*, a Wild Horizons Postcard Book, P.O. Box 5118–00, Tucson, Arizona 85703–0118 USA
Photo © 1991 by Thomas Wiewandt.

COMMON FROM TEXAS to southern California and northern Mexico, the ocotillo (*Fouquieria splendens*) is sometimes called the hygrometer of the desert. Within days after a rain, its thorny stems — naked most of the year to conserve moisture — sprout a lush coat of leaves. As the soil dries, its leaves promptly turn yellow and fall off. (1700)

From *DESERT RAIN/DESERT BLOOM*, a Wild Horizons Postcard Book, P.O. Box 5118–00, Tucson, Arizona 85703–0118 USA
Photo © 1991 by Thomas Wiewandt.

SUMMER RAINS BRING a vivid display of flowering mules-ears (*Wyethia scabra*) to the Coral Pink Sand Dunes State Reserve in the Great Basin Desert of southern Utah. (1800)

From *DESERT RAIN/DESERT BLOOM*, a Wild Horizons Postcard Book, P.O. Box 5118–00, Tucson, Arizona 85703–0118 USA
Photo © 1991 by Thomas Wiewandt.

A S WINTER REACHES Utah's Coral Pink Sand Dunes State Reserve, floral skeletons of *Wyethia scabra* remind us of summer's bounty. A beetle has passed by in the night. (1900)

From *DESERT RAIN*/*DESERT BLOOM*, a Wild Horizons Postcard Book, P.O. Box 5118–00, Tucson, Arizona 85703–0118 USA
Photo © 1991 by Thomas Wiewandt.

O N RARE OCCASIONS, winter fog blankets southern Arizona's forest of saguaro cacti (*Carnegiea gigantea*) and paloverde trees (*Cercidium microphyllum*). In contrast to summer's show of boisterous storms, called "male rains" by the Navajo, the "female rains" of winter are slow and soaking. (2000)

From *DESERT RAIN/DESERT BLOOM*, a Wild Horizons Postcard Book, P.O. Box 5118–00, Tucson, Arizona 85703–0118 USA
Photo © 1991 by Thomas Wiewandt.

W HEN RAIN TURNS to snow, the Sonoran Desert foothills of southern Arizona become a wonderland of unexpected gentleness and beauty. These desert plants of tropical origin experience snowfalls of several inches once every 10–15 years. (2100)

From *DESERT RAIN/DESERT BLOOM*, a Wild Horizons Postcard Book, P.O. Box 5118–00, Tucson, Arizona 85703–0118 USA
Photo © 1991 by Thomas Wiewandt.

ABOUT THE AUTHOR-PHOTOGRAPHER

AS A CHILD in northern New Mexico, Tom Wiewandt formed a deep and lasting spiritual connection with the natural world—from the lashing power of a summer storm to such small dramas as a fence lizard doing push-ups on a log.

Armed with a mastery of photography and a Ph.D. in ecology, Tom wants to pique our curiosity and sense of wonder. He blends art and science in a tapestry of images that stir our imaginations and make us long to see more. DESERT RAIN/DESERT BLOOM is drawn from his years of exploring the colors and contrasts of the desert Southwest.

Tom's camera has brought the mysteries of things wild to the pages of *Audubon, Smithsonian, Omni,* and *National Wildlife.* His first trade book, HIDDEN LIFE OF THE DESERT (Crown/Random House, 1990), made the John Burroughs List of Outstanding Nature Books for Young Readers. Because life doesn't stand still, Tom has captured the dynamics of animal behavior and the world around us in his films for the BBC and the National Geographic Society. He also invites others to experience the lure of field photography on his Wild Horizons Photographic Safaris, where participants learn to interact with nature from both sides of the camera.

Other Postcard Books from Wild Horizons Publishing:

CACTUS FLOWERS by Thomas Wiewandt (ISBN 1-879728-01-X)

Although short-lived, cactus flowers are well worth waiting for, clearly exemplified by the fiesta of color in this book. Their stunning beauty has been captured on film, in 21 extraordinary close-up images. Includes an overview of the cactus family.

ANCIENT SEA CREATURES by Thomas Wiewandt (ISBN 1-879728-02-8)

A fresh view of the past, through photographic close-ups of fossils selected and composed to fire the imagination: trilobites, ammonites, sea-lilies, fish, and more. Includes an overview of the early history of life on Earth and an easy-to-understand geologic time clock.

. . . .

Wild Horizons Photographic Safaris:

Since 1985, Wild Horizons has been offering 1- to 3-week learning vacations in nature photography. These first-class, all-inclusive travel packages cater to groups of 4–8 participants and feature scenic destinations in the American West and abroad. We specialize in customized tours for small groups, arranged at least a year in advance.

For more information, please return the enclosed order form.